Let's Play

A Social Connection
Book Game

2nd Edition

Robert Jason Grant

AutPlay® Publishing

Let's Play: A Social Connection Book Game
2nd Edition

©2016, ©2020 Robert Jason Grant Ed.D
Springfield, Missouri: AutPlay® Publishing
A Robert Jason Grant Ed.D Product

ISBN: 978-1-7329099-1-5

All Images Provided by ClipArtLord.com unless otherwise noted.

Correspondence regarding this book:
AutPlay® Publishing
info@autplaytherapy.com
www.autplaytherapy.com

For Nolan

"Life is more fun if you play games."
— Roald Dahl

About This Book Game

Let's Play: A Social Connection Book Game is a creatively designed game in book form. Therapists, school counselors, parents, and other professionals working with children and adolescents can utilize this book to play, interact, and improve connection and relationship development. *Let's Play* follows an integrative psychoeducational model incorporating elements of directive, humanistic, and developmental/attachment theories and processes. *Let's Play* utilizes influences from play therapy with an underlying focus on relationship development between professional/parent and child. The variety of experience and activity in *Let's Play* allows for addressing a plethora of relationship related needs.

Professionals can use *Let's Play* as a rapport building tool by introducing the book game to their clients and playfully engaging in each page. The professional plays with the child thus listening to the child's responses and reflecting feelings and beliefs. The professional also shares their own responses, providing the opportunity for modeling. *Let's Play* can also serve as an assessment tool allowing professionals to gain insight and information about the child or adolescent – their families, their thoughts and feelings, likes and dislikes. It functions as a useful resource for both individual and family therapy. As a structured intervention, *Let's Play* can be incorporated into therapy planning to help address a variety of potential needs, including the following:

- Anxiety reduction and communication
- Social navigation/interaction comfort
- Engagement and attachment needs
- Sensory and regulation challenges
- Relationship development
- Parent/child relationship strain

About Social Navigation

The term social navigation actually functions as an umbrella term, covering a wide scope and variety of social related awareness, strengths, needs, and experiences which range from simple to more complex.

Social situations and interactions can create anxiety and dysregulation for some children. Social situations can be confusing as the social rules or expectations can vary from one person to another, environment to another, culture to another. Often there are hidden rules – things that are understood by many in a particular environment but would not be clear to someone new to the environment. Often social expectations can seem contradictory and do not make logical sense, for example, telling a child to work on "not ignoring others" and the very next day to work on "ignoring a particular child." Many social expectations involve a great deal of nuance which can be confusing.

A child's specific social needs should be carefully assessed and always addressed through a neurodiversity affirming process. If possible, the child should have a clear voice in communicating what they believe their social needs are and what they would like to work on.

The social navigation focus of this book is designed to help children feel more comfortable and confident interacting with another person. The format is constructed to present a playful approach and atmosphere as children become more empowered in their social navigation. Children should not be forced to participate in the book game or in any of the components if they do not feel comfortable.

About Connection and Relationship Development

A lack of connection or being able to feel a true sense of relationship may be one of the most troubling concerns for children; especially in the parent/child relationship. Connection and relationship development cannot be considered without a focus on the parent/child relationship.

This is the beginning and essence of the development of these constructs.

What is happening between child and parent cannot be undervalued. Parent and child need to feel connection between themselves as the child utilizes the healthy parent/child connection to reach out and explore connection in other ways with other people. Often children establish closeness with others in which they feel safe. In this relationship, they will seek support from adults with whom they trust and show enjoyment in their close relationships.

When children can establish closeness with others, a sense of connection and safety being with others, and support and comfort from others, they are more likely to development healthy relationships and healthy interaction skills throughout their lifetime.

The connection and relationship development focus in this book is designed to increase connection between child and parent and increase relationship development between child and other significant relationships. The connection component is also designed to teach children and adolescents how to be more successful in engaging others and increasing relationship connections while providing a fun, natural, play based atmosphere for children and adolescents to master greater relationship and connection.

Using Let's Play with Children and Adolescents

Let's Play is appropriate for use with children and adolescents from approximately 5 years old to 18. The book game can be utilized by professionals to address therapy goals or by parents who are engaging in a special play time or activity with their child.

Each page of this book begins by playing one of ten engaging connection activities. The connection activities include: Rock, Paper, Scissors, Thumb Wrestle, Staring Game (don't blink), Patty Cake Categories, Freeze (don't move), Feelings Face Off, In Which Hand, Arm Wrestle,

Make Me Laugh, and Best Move. Whoever wins the activity chooses from a list of five interactive options. The winner decides what they will do, and what the other person playing the game will do.

The five interactive options are: answer the question, top 3, what if, complete the sentence, and do this. Players should start on the first page of play and continue through the end of the book game. There are 60 game play pages. *Let's Play* book game can be played repeatedly, going through the book game multiple times with different interactive options chosen to complete.

Professionals and parents can have a fun and engaging experience with children and adolescents through the connection activities and can ask follow up questions and role model when participating in the interactive options. Children and adolescents who might benefit from this book game include those struggling with communication and relationship development, social anxiety, emotion regulation and engagement, attachment issues, and parent/child relationship issues.

Instructions

How to Play

Let's Play is designed for two players but may be adapted for up to four players for family therapy work.

Players start with the first play page.

The players complete a connection activity. Whoever wins the connection activity then chooses what both players will do from the five interactive options listed on the page.

For example, the professional and an 8-year-old child are playing *Let's Play*. They are on a page which starts with the connection activity *Rock, Paper, Scissors*. They play the game and the child wins. The child then chooses from the 5 interactive options which they will do and what the professional will so. The child chooses to answer the *what if* question and tells the professional they must do *complete the sentence.*

Once the interactive options have been completed, the players move to the next page following the same instructions.

There are 60 total game pages to complete. If professionals and parents get through all 60 play pages, they should play again being mindful to choose new interactive options to complete.

Addressing Competition, Who Should Win?

It will be important to explain that "winning" the connection activities is not the priority. The connection games should be fun and connecting. If it is within the professional or parents' control, the ideal situation would be that the professional or parent wins some of the games and the child wins some of the games. There may be a situation where the child wins all the games which is fine. There should not be an emphasis on winning the connection games.

The Ten Connection Activities (games) Explained

1. Rock Paper Scissors
   A hand game played between two people, in which each player on the count of three simultaneously forms one of three shapes with an outstretched hand. These shapes are "rock" (a simple fist), "paper" (a flat hand), and "scissors" (a fist with the index and middle fingers together forming a V). The game has three possible outcomes other than a tie: a player who decides to play rock will beat another player who has chosen scissors ("rock crushes scissors") but will lose to one who has played paper ("paper covers rock"); a play of paper will lose to a play of scissors ("scissors cut paper"). If both players choose the same shape, the game is tied and is replayed to break the tie. The game can be played once or best out of three.

2. Thumb Wrestle

   In this game, two players lock fingers with one hand. They lay their thumbs on top of their closed fist. On the count of three each person taps their thumb on alternating sides of their fists looking for the opportunity to pin their opponent's thumb under their own. The first person to pin the other person's thumb is the winner.

3. Staring Game (do not blink)

   This is a staring contest where two people stare at each other making eye contact until one person blinks or looks away. The first person to blink or look away loses the contest.

4. Patty Cake Categories

   A simple hand clapping game played with two people; hands are clapped in a standard crisscross motion with each other in a comfortable rhythm. In Patty Cake Categories, an additional instruction is added to the simple hand clapping game. While the players are hand clapping, they must keep naming things from a pre-chosen category such as emotions, animals, fruits, or sports (the adult and child can decide together what category they want to use before the game begins). There can be no repeats and once someone is unable to think of anything to say or repeats what has already been said, the game is over. The first person to repeat something that has already been said, or cannot think of anything to say, loses the game.

5. Freeze (do not move)

   Players must freeze their whole body and face. Players must remain frozen until one of the players moves, whoever moves first loses the game.

6. Feelings Face Off

   One player begins by naming an emotion. The next player then names a different emotion. Play moves back and forth with each player naming a different emotion until one player repeats an emotion that has already been said or cannot think of anything to say. The first person to repeat an emotion or cannot think of anything to say loses the game. This game can also be played using paper and taking turns writing the emotions down.

7. In Which Hand

   Each person picks something small like a penny, a marble, a rolled-up piece of paper, etc. and places it in one of their hands (making a fist). This should be done so the other person does not see which hand the item was put in. Once both people have done this, they try to guess which hand the item is in. Whoever guesses correctly is the winner. If both people guess correctly, they play again until there is a winner.

8. Arm Wrestle

   The two players sit at a table across from each other. They each place one elbow/arm on the table and clasp each other's hand in a handshake type grip. Someone says "Go" and they each try to pin the other persons arm to the table. Whoever pins the other persons arm is the winner.

9. Make Me Laugh

   Both people face each other, and one person says "Go." Each person is trying to do something to make the other person laugh first. They can do body movements, tell jokes, make faces, or whatever they want to do to try and make the other person laugh. Whoever laughs first is the loser.

10. Best Move

Each person gets to think of a special move to do. Each person performs their move for the other person. Together, they must decide who had the best move. The person with the best move is the winner.

The ten connection activities are designed to be fun and playful. Professionals and parents should make this part of the book game fun and enjoyable for the child or adolescent. These activities are simple and require no props, yet they create an engagement between the adult and child and promote attachment and social interaction. If the professional or parent are able to win every game, the professional or parent should let the child or adolescent win some of the games so that the child or adolescent has the opportunity to choose some of the interactive options. This book game works best when both the adult and the child win some of the connection games, and thus each can contribute to choosing some of the interactive options.

The Five Interactive Options Explained

1. Answer the question – This option simply asks a question such as "How do you like to play?" or When do you feel happy?" The questions should be fully answered avoiding one-word responses.
2. Say your top three – This option gives a category and asks the person to name their top three things in the category such as favorite school subjects or things about your home. The answer does not have to be a ranking but can be if the person chooses to answer this way.
3. What if – This option presents scenarios and the person must respond to the scenario such as what if there were no more computers or what if you moved to another state?

4. Complete the sentence – This option begins a sentence that needs to be completed. The person must try to fully complete the sentence. An example would be – Being happy means…
5. Do this – This option is about action. A movement or activity is presented, and the person must do it. Some examples would be – act like an animal, twist your body like a pretzel, and act like you are climbing a tree.

The five interactive options vary from questions to completing tasks. These interactive options provide opportunity to work on social navigation, engaging with another person, improving communication, practicing sensory processing activities, improving emotional regulation and awareness, strengthening rapport and relationship, gathering assessment information, and simply having fun. The professional or parent will want to guide the book game ensuring a playful atmosphere while maintaining focus on therapy needs.

Try Some Additional Connection Activities (games) Just for Fun!

Create a Special Handshake
Create your own special handshake by making up moves only you and the other person know. Do not pick so many elements that you cannot remember the sequence and practice it a lot. The more effortless the handshake seems, the better.

Shadow Puppets
All you need is a bright light and a blank wall. Using your hands and placing them in front of the light, reflect images (puppets) onto the wall. Do your best bird or butterfly impression, and make sure that you and the child engage together to create shadow puppets or tell a puppet story. Need some inspiration? Check out this website of manual manipulations: shadow-puppets.com.

Hand Slaps
Despite its name, you do not have to slap or play the game so hard that

it is hurtful. Start by placing your hands out in front of you, palms up. Have the child place their hands, palms down, on top of yours. Your hands should not rest against each other but should just barely touch as they hover in midair. Your objective is to quickly bring your hands around your opponent's and tap the backs of their hands. Your opponent tries to anticipate this maneuver, pulling their hands away to avoid the tap. If you can tap the other side of your opponent's hands three times before you miss, you win. If the opponent avoids your tap, then you switch positions and they try to tap your hands.

Hand Tracing

The two players hold hands, while one of them closes their eyes. The second player will trace an alphabet, number, or for older children or adolescents, small words, onto the hand of the player whose eyes are closed. This player will need to guess what is being traced onto his or her hand using only their sense of touch. If successful, he or she wins, otherwise, the person who finger-traced is the winner.

Hand Stacking

Take turns stacking hands one on top of the other, place one of your hands out, the child places one of their hands on top of your hand, you place your other hand on top of the child's hand, they place their other hand on top of yours and you keep moving the bottom hand to the top. You can continue this game to stack hands as high as the kids can reach. You can also go low and stack hands downwards.

Fist Stacking

Similar to the hand stacking game, you can stack your fists. Each player makes a fist and takes turn stacking their fists higher and higher. The fist at the bottom of the stack goes next and play continues until you can't reach any higher. You can also go low and stack fists backward. You can make several variations (slow motion, fast) and create your own special way to stack.

High Five Games

Give a high five multiple ways. Possible positions include a high five, low five, high ten, low ten, one hand high and one hand low, two hands far apart, crisscross high fives, or crisscross low fives. You can also do them in slow motion or do them fast. You can be creative and come up with different positions.

What Number

One person goes first and using their fingers, displays a number between 1-10 behind their back. The other person must guess the number and they get three tries. If they guess the number, they get to go, and the other person has to try and guess. If they do not guess in three tries, they must try again with a new number.

Palm Press Follow

The players press their palms against each other. One person starts as the leader and leads them both around the room, their palms must stay pressed together. After a while, they switch so the other person leads.

Mirroring

The adult and child take turns mirroring each other's moves.

Pretend Palm Reading

The adult has the child hold out one of their hands palm up. The adult gives the child a playful palm reading. The adult takes their index finger and traces different lines in the child's palm and has each line be something different such as their play line, their always a good helper line, their funny line, etc.

Holding Hands House Tour

The parent and child pick a starting point in their house and hold hands. They must walk throughout the whole house, touring every room, while they keep holding hands. For extra fun, they can try going through the house with both hands held. They can also play the game outside.

Let's Play

Rock, Paper, Scissors

(Winner chooses who does what below)

Answer the Question

Who is the funniest person in your family?

Say Your Top 3

Worst foods

What If

Your best friend moved in with you?

Complete the Sentence

I am calm when…

Do This

Run in place for 5 seconds

Let's Play

Thumb Wrestle

(Winner chooses who does what below)

Answer the Question

Have you ever felt uncomfortable around other kids?

Say Your Top 3

Favorite family members

What If

You had to wear a uniform everyday?

Complete the Sentence

One day I will…

Do This

Laugh

Let's Play

Staring Game (don't blink)

(Winner chooses who does what below)

Answer the Question

Have you ever helped someone else?

Say Your Top 3

Fun places to go

What If

You lived by yourself?

Complete the Sentence

When I am mad I…

Do This

Stand up and touch your fingers to your toes

Let's Play

Patty Cake Categories

(Winner chooses who does what below)

Answer the Question

What is a favorite trip you have been on?

Say Your Top 3

Things to do with your family

What If

You could only eat one food the rest of your life?

Complete the Sentence

School is…

Do This

Give someone a high five

Let's Play

Freeze (don't move)

(Winner chooses who does what below)

Answer the Question

Who is the weirdest person in your family?

Say Your Top 3

Wishes for your future

What If

You felt mad all the time?

Complete the Sentence

The worst thing that could happen is…

Do This

Count to ten slowly

Let's Play

Feelings Face Off

(Winner chooses who does what below)

Answer the Question

What are the names of your friends?

Say Your Top 3

Things that make you feel happy

What If

Someone gave you $100?

Complete the Sentence

My best quality is…

Do This

Act like you're playing a sport

Let's Play

In Which Hand

(Winner chooses who does what below)

Answer the Question

What is your favorite toy or game?

Say Your Top 3

Holidays

What If

You felt sad all the time?

Complete the Sentence

Dear parents…

Do This

Give yourself a body hug

Let's Play

Arm Wrestle

(Winner chooses who does what below)

Answer the Question

How do you like to play?

Say Your Top 3

Restaurants

What If

A new kid at school wanted to sit by you at lunch?

Complete the Sentence

I wish I could…

Do This

Make a confused face

Let's Play

Make Me Laugh

(Winner chooses who does what below)

Answer the Question

When do you feel happy?

Say Your Top 3

Worst chores

What If

You had to do chores all day long?

Complete the Sentence

Teachers are…

Do This

Pretend you are punching a punching bag

Let's Play

Best Move

(Winner chooses who does what below)

Answer the Question

How would you change your family?

Say Your Top 3

Favorite school subjects

What If

You never went to school?

Complete the Sentence

Bullies are…

Do This

Walk in slow motion around the room

Let's Play

Rock, Paper, Scissors

(Winner chooses who does what below)

Answer the Question

When do you feel calm?

Say Your Top 3

Things you wish you had

What If

Every kid at school wanted to be your friend?

Complete the Sentence

People think I am…

Do This

Jump as high as you can

Let's Play

Thumb Wrestle

(Winner chooses who does what below)

Answer the Question

When do you feel worried?

Say Your Top 3

Teachers

What If

You didn't have parents?

Complete the Sentence

My safe place is…

Do This

Pretend like you're playing the drums

Let's Play

Staring Game (don't blink)

(Winner chooses who does what below)

Answer the Question

Do you like school?

Say Your Top 3

Things someone can do if they are bullied

What If

You could do whatever you wanted?

Complete the Sentence

My greatest accomplishment is…

Do This

Spin around 3 times

Let's Play

Patty Cake Categories

(Winner chooses who does what below)

Answer the Question

When do you feel confident?

Say Your Top 3

Scary things

What If

Your family moved to another state?

Complete the Sentence

I think about…

Do This

Act like an animal

Let's Play

Freeze (don't move)

(Winner chooses who does what below)

Answer the Question

When was a time you felt sorry?

Say Your Top 3

Favorite things about school

What If

Other kids asked you to play with them?

Complete the Sentence

Being happy means…

Do This

Pretend you are an airplane flying around the room

Let's Play

Feelings Face Off

(Winner chooses who does what below)

Answer the Question

How would you change yourself?

Say Your Top 3

Toys

What If

You were the most popular kid in school?

Complete the Sentence

I am sad when…

Do This

Tell a joke

Let's Play

In Which Hand

(Winner chooses who does what below)

Answer the Question

Have you ever been bullied?

Say Your Top 3

Things that make you mad

What If

You became a professional athlete?

Complete the Sentence

I wish my parents would…

Do This

Act like you are swimming

Let's Play

Arm Wrestle

(Winner chooses who does what below)

Answer the Question

What is one of your favorite things to do?

Say Your Top 3

Feelings

What If

School lasted all year long?

Complete the Sentence

I am scared of…

Do This

Walk backwards around the room

Let's Play

Make Me Laugh

(Winner chooses who does what below)

Answer the Question

Do you think kids should participate in groups or clubs?

Say Your Top 3

Things that make you feel calm

What If

Someone designed a video game based on your life?

Complete the Sentence

Dear Dad…

Do This

Take 3 deep breaths

Let's Play

Best Move

(Winner chooses who does what below)

Answer the Question

What is the worst quality a person can have?

Say Your Top 3

Sports

What If

Someone wrote a book about your family?

Complete the Sentence

People don't like it when I…

Do This

Hop on one foot around the room

Let's Play

Rock, Paper, Scissors

(Winner chooses who does what below)

Answer the Question

What do you think is the best quality a person can have?

Say Your Top 3

Ways kids get bullied

What If

Everyone in school was invited to a party except you?

Complete the Sentence

When I play I...

Do This

Make an angry face

Let's Play

Thumb Wrestle

(Winner chooses who does what below)

Answer the Question

Who in your family is most like you?

Say Your Top 3

Favorite video or computer games

What If

You had to stay in your room for 3 days?

Complete the Sentence

I am good at…

Do This

Act like you are playing a video game

Let's Play

Staring Game (don't blink)

(Winner chooses who does what below)

Answer the Question

What are some reasons that kids should attend school?

Say Your Top 3

People you would like to be friends with

What If

Your favorite toy got destroyed?

Complete the Sentence

I feel confused when…

Do This

Pretend like you are crawling through a cave

Let's Play

Patty Cake Categories

(Winner chooses who does what below)

Answer the Question

What is something you like to do with other kids?

Say Your Top 3

Things that make you nervous

What If

You had to act in a play?

Complete the Sentence

My parents are…

Do This

Make a silly face

Let's Play

Freeze (don't move)

(Winner chooses who does what below)

Answer the Question

What is the hardest part about being in school?

Say Your Top 3

Bad memories

What If

Everyone you knew had a party for you?

Complete the Sentence

Dear Mom…

Do This

Create a special handshake

Let's Play

Feelings Face Off

(Winner chooses who does what below)

Answer the Question

Has there been a time you have felt rejected or left out?

Say Your Top 3

Movies or TV shows

What If

There were no more computers?

Complete the Sentence

Friends are…

Do This

5 jumping jacks

Let's Play

In Which Hand

(Winner chooses who does what below)

Answer the Question

How would you describe yourself?

Say Your Top 3

Things about your home

What If

You lost all your hair?

Complete the Sentence

I don't like…

Do This

Act like you are blowing up a balloon

Let's Play

Arm Wrestle

(Winner chooses who does what below)

Answer the Question

What is something you have done to be a good friend?

Say Your Top 3

Musical Instruments

What If

Your eyes changed color?

Complete the Sentence

When I get worried I…

Do This

Twist your body like a pretzel

Let's Play

Make Me Laugh

(Winner chooses who does what below)

Answer the Question

How would you describe your school?

Say Your Top 3

Best things about you

What If

Someone tried to scare you?

Complete the Sentence

Everyone in my family…

Do This

Act like you are climbing a tree

Let's Play

Best Move

(Winner chooses who does what below)

Answer the Question

When you get upset, what do you do?

Say Your Top 3

Favorite animals

What If

There were no rules?

Complete the Sentence

When I am an adult I will…

Do This

Pretend like you are relaxing

Let's Play

Rock, Paper, Scissors

(Winner chooses who does what below)

Answer the Question

What animal would you choose as a pet?

Say Your Top 3

Pets you would like to have

What If

You got to make all the rules?

Complete the Sentence

I'm embarrassed when…

Do This

A karate move

Let's Play

Thumb Wrestle

(Winner chooses who does what below)

Answer the Question

What makes you feel important?

Say Your Top 3

Desserts

What If

Your parents got angry with you?

Complete the Sentence

Sometimes I wish…

Do This

Dance

Let's Play

Staring Game (don't blink)

(Winner chooses who does what below)

Answer the Question

Have you ever wanted to run away?

Say Your Top 3

Dinosaurs

What If

There were no more cars?

Complete the Sentence

You might not know…

Do This

Act like your eating a carrot

Let's Play

Patty Cake Categories

(Winner chooses who does what below)

Answer the Question

Have you ever won an award?

Say Your Top 3

Cartoons

What If

You had your own robot?

Complete the Sentence

I hate doing…

Do This

Act like your eating peanut butter

Let's Play

Freeze (don't move)

(Winner chooses who does what below)

Answer the Question

How do you think people stay happy?

Say Your Top 3

Mythical creatures

What If

Everyone thought you were weird?

Complete the Sentence

A favorite memory is…

Do This

Act like your rowing a boat

Let's Play

Feelings Face Off

(Winner chooses who does what below)

Answer the Question

Who would help you with a problem?

Say Your Top 3

Worst smells

What If

Someone lied to you?

Complete the Sentence

I like it when…

Do This

Act like your ice skating

Let's Play

In Which Hand

(Winner chooses who does what below)

Answer the Question

How do people learn new things?

Say Your Top 3

Cars

What If

Schools didn't have lunch?

Complete the Sentence

I feel comfortable when…

Do This

Stand on one foot for 10 seconds

Let's Play

Arm Wrestle

(Winner chooses who does what below)

Answer the Question

What do kids like to do the most?

Say Your Top 3

Things to do on a rainy day

What If

No one ever taught you anything?

Complete the Sentence

New things…

Do This

Make a scared face

Let's Play

Make Me Laugh

(Winner chooses who does what below)

Answer the Question

What do you not like to talk about?

Say Your Top 3

Drinks

What If

You became a monster?

Complete the Sentence

A great invention would be?

Do This

Make a proud face

Let's Play

Best Move

(Winner chooses who does what below)

Answer the Question

Why do you think people are mean?

Say Your Top 3

Things to buy in a store.

What If

Someone broke a promise?

Complete the Sentence

I think sports are…

Do This

Pretend you're a tree

Let's Play

Rock, Paper, Scissors

(Winner chooses who does what below)

Answer the Question

Do you think you will be famous one day?

Say Your Top 3

Places in your house

What If

Your friends teased you?

Complete the Sentence

I think art is…

Do This

Act like you are digging a hole in the ground

Let's Play

Thumb Wrestle

(Winner chooses who does what below)

Answer the Question

Do you ever think about your future?

Say Your Top 3

Summer activities

What If

You became president?

Complete the Sentence

Adults are…

Do This

Make a worried face

Let's Play

Staring Game (don't blink)

(Winner chooses who does what below)

Answer the Question

Have you ever visited another country?

Say Your Top 3

Chores to avoid

What If

Parents bought their kids everything they wanted?

Complete the Sentence

Something I never wanted to do is…

Do This

Pat your head and rub your tummy

Let's Play

Patty Cake Categories

(Winner chooses who does what below)

Answer the Question

What makes you feel confused?

Say Your Top 3

Things to do outside

What If

Video game characters were real?

Complete the Sentence

I am tired of people…

Do This

Make animal noises

Let's Play

Freeze (don't move)

(Winner chooses who does what below)

Answer the Question

Would you rather play Minecraft or checkers?

Say Your Top 3

Things about your city

What If

Playing was against the law?

Complete the Sentence

I can…

Do This

Pretend you are cutting your own hair

Let's Play

Feelings Face Off

(Winner chooses who does what below)

Answer the Question

Have you ever taken a walk in the woods?

Say Your Top 3

Favorite clothes

What If

Everyone colored their hair purple?

Complete the Sentence

When I am alone…

Do This

Trace the lines on the palm of your hand

Let's Play

In Which Hand

(Winner chooses who does what below)

Answer the Question

Would you rather play in a park or play Roblox?

Say Your Top 3

Things about your life

What If

Dogs could talk?

Complete the Sentence

A good time would be…

Do This

Make a pinky promise

Let's Play

Arm Wrestle

(Winner chooses who does what below)

Answer the Question

What makes people feel sad?

Say Your Top 3

Ways to play

What If

You could wish for one thing and get it?

Complete the Sentence

I smile when…

Do This

Pretend you are building something

Let's Play

Make Me Laugh

(Winner chooses who does what below)

Answer the Question

Do you have any special abilities?

Say Your Top 3

Surprises

What If

People asked you questions all the time?

Complete the Sentence

I feel happy when…

Do This

Pretend you are a statue

Let's Play

Best Move

(Winner chooses who does what below)

Answer the Question

What makes you feel confused?

Say Your Top 3

Confusing Things

What If

No one ever talked to you?

Complete the Sentence

My favorite place is…

Do This

Shake your whole body

Let's Play Again!

About Dr. Robert Jason Grant

Dr. Grant is a Licensed Professional Counselor, National Certified Counselor, and Registered Play Therapist Supervisor. Dr. Grant specializes in working with children, adolescents, and families, including working with neurodivergent children (autism, ADHD, sensory differences, learning disorders, and developmental disabilities). He is the creator of AutPlay® Therapy, an integrative family play therapy framework designed to help address the mental health needs of neurodivergent children and adolescents. He is also trained in EMDR (Eye Movement Desensitization and Reprocessing) Therapy, a Post Traumatic Stress Disorder/trauma related therapy for children and adults.

Dr. Grant utilizes several years of clinical experience and his own lived neurodivergent experience to work with children and their families. Dr. Grant is committed to provided affirming resources to help address the mental health needs of neurodivergent children and their families. He owns and operates the AutPlay® Therapy Clinic in Southwest Missouri, providing play therapy, trauma informed therapy, and educational resources for the neurodivergent population.

Dr. Grant is an international speaker and keynote presenter having presented for the American Counseling Association, Association for Play Therapy, American Mental Health Counselors Association, and The World Autism Congress. He is a multi-published author of several articles, book chapters, and books.

Dr. Grant is currently serving as the chair on the board of directors for the Association for Play Therapy. He is also a part time instructor in the Play Therapy Certificate program at Mid America Nazarene University (MNU).

Additional Products by Dr. Robert Jason Grant

● *Understanding Autism: A Neurodiversity Affirming Guidebook for Children and Teens*

● *The AutPlay® Therapy Handbook: Integrative Family Play Therapy for Neurodivergent Children*

● *Play-Based Interventions for Autism Spectrum Disorder and Other Developmental Disabilities*

● *Understanding Sensory Differences: A Neurodiversity Affirming Guidebook for Children and Teens*

● *Understanding ADHD: A Neurodiversity Affirming Guidebook for Children and Teens*

● *AutPlay® Therapy Play and Social Skill Groups: A 10 Session Model*

● *Play Therapy Theories and Perspectives: Diversity of Thought in the Field*

Learn more about Dr. Robert Jason Grant and inquire about the trainings, products, and therapy he offers at www.robertjasongrant.com and www.autplaytherapy.com.

You may also connect with Dr. Grant though Facebook, LinkedIn, and YouTube.

www.robertjasongrant.com

www.autplaytherapy.com